ANIMAL ENGINEERS

Weavers

by Rebecca Pettiford

BLASTOFF! READERS 3

BELLWETHER MEDIA • MINNEAPOLIS, MN

Blastoff! Readers are carefully developed by literacy experts to build reading stamina and move students toward fluency by combining standards-based content with developmentally appropriate text.

Level 1 provides the most support through repetition of high-frequency words, light text, predictable sentence patterns, and strong visual support.

Level 2 offers early readers a bit more challenge through varied sentences, increased text load, and text-supportive special features.

Level 3 advances early-fluent readers toward fluency through increased text load, less reliance on photos, advancing concepts, longer sentences, and more complex special features.

★ **Blastoff! Universe**

This edition first published in 2025 by Bellwether Media, Inc.

Library of Congress Cataloging-in-Publication Data

LLC record for Weavers available at: https://lccn.loc.gov/2024015035

Editor: Rachael Barnes Designer: Josh Brink

Printed in the United States of America, North Mankato, MN.

Table of Contents

Weaving Nests

Weavers are small birds. They are the only birds that tie knots!

Males **weave** large, roofed nests to try to win a **mate**. The nests also keep weavers safe from **predators**.

nest

There are more than 120 weaver **species**. Most live in Africa. Others live in Asia and Australia.

baya weaver

Baya Weaver Range Map

From **savannas** to **wetlands**, weavers can live in many different **habitats**. Their nests come in different shapes and sizes.

Planning a Nest

Before male weavers find a mate, they choose a site for their nests. Many species pick sites near or over water.

Weavers pick areas where food is plentiful. They also look for spots close to nest building supplies.

Weavers use grasses, leaves, and twigs to build their nests. Most species build single nests.

Sociable weavers make huge community nests. Hundreds of weaver pairs can live in one nest!

Time to Weave!

A male weaver uses his cone-shaped beak to tear off strips of plants. He ties one onto a thin tree branch.

He holds the top of the strip in his beak. He holds the bottom part with his **talons**.

He ties a knot with his beak.
This knot supports the entire nest.
Once the knot is tight, he makes
a ring from more strips.

He continues building from the roof down.

The male weaves together hundreds of plant strips. He pulls them with his beak over and under one another.

Building Materials

grasses

leaves

twigs

Finally, he weaves the narrow entrance. He builds it just large enough for weavers to enter.

The Nest Is Ready!

Weaver nests are safe.
Their entrances make it hard
for predators to get inside.

Most nest entrances face down. Some weavers add a tunnel to the entrance. Other weavers build fake entrances to trick predators!

The male **flutters** his wings. A female sees him and his **stable** nest. She flies into his nest. He has won a mate!

Some weavers reuse their nest sites. They remove their last nest and start again!

Identify Weaver Nests

- you can tell which species built a nest by looking at its size and shape

baya weaver

sociable weaver

southern masked weaver

white-browed sparrow weaver

Glossary

flutters—to move quickly up and down in the air

habitats—the natural homes of plants and animals

mate—one of a breeding pair of animals

predators—animals that hunt other animals for food

savannas—grasslands in warm areas that have few trees

species—kinds of animals

stable—not easily changed or destroyed

talons—sharp claws on birds that allow them to grab and tear

weave—to form by passing strips of materials over and under each other

wetlands—areas of land that are covered with low levels of water for most of the year

To Learn More

AT THE LIBRARY

Mayntz, Melissa. *Birds for Kids: A Junior Scientist's Guide to Owls, Eagles, Penguins, and Other Bird Species.* Naperville, Ill.: Callisto Publishing, 2024.

Pettiford, Rebecca. *Bowerbirds.* Minneapolis, Minn.: Bellwether Media, 2025.

Rouse, Dan. *The Children's Book of Birdwatching.* New York, N.Y.: DK Publishing, 2023.

ON THE WEB

FACTSURFER

Factsurfer.com gives you a safe, fun way to find more information.

1. Go to www.factsurfer.com.
2. Enter "weavers" into the search box and click 🔍.
3. Select your book cover to see a list of related content.

Index

The images in this book are reproduced through the courtesy of: PACO COMO, cover, back cover, p. 16; Henk Bogaard, p. 3; Platoo Studio, p. 4; tahirsphotography, pp. 4-5; Thanit Weerawan, pp. 6-7; Peter Mullineux, pp. 8-9; Ken Griffiths, p. 9; tristan tan, pp. 10, 23; Christine Cuthbertson/ Alamy, p. 11; Maximiliane Wagner, pp. 12-13; Butterfly Hunter, p. 13 (feature bird and talons); Tobie Oosthuizen, p. 14; Rich Carey, p. 15; Ann and Steve Toon/ Alamy, p. 17 (twigs); joesayhello/ iStock, p. 17 (leaves); Alistair Homer, p. 17 (grasses); Independent birds, pp. 18-19; tee262, p. 20; Tom Wurl, p. 21 (sociable weaver); Singha Songsak P, p. 21 (baya weaver); David Wall/ Alamy, p. 21 (southern masked weaver); Ivica Gulija/ iStock, p. 21 (white-barrowed sparrow weaver); Jen Watson, pp. 20-21.